Michelangelo and Raphael drawings

Catherine Whistler

Sponsored by
Christie's Fine Art Auctioneers
London

Phaidon · Christie's Limited
in association
with the Ashmolean Museum

First published 1990
Phaidon · Christie's Limited
Musterlin House, Jordan Hill Road, Oxford OX2 8DP

Published in association with the Ashmolean Museum
Text and illustrations (c) Ashmolean Museum, Oxford 1990
Published in paperback by the Ashmolean Museum, 1990

ISBN 0 7148 8079 5 (hardback)
1 85444 002 0 (paperback)

A CIP record for this book is available from the British
Library

Jacket illustrations: (front) Michelangelo, Ideal head, plate
26; (back) Raphael, A group of four standing soldiers,
plate 2

Designed by Cole design unit, Reading
Set in Versailles by Meridian Phototypesetting Limited
Printed and bound in Great Britain by
Jolly & Barber Limited, Rugby

Raphael *Head of a youth,
possibly a self-portrait.*
Grey-black chalk,
heightened with white,
on faded white paper.
38.1 × 26.1 cm. P.II 515.

Introduction

In many ways, two artists less alike than Raphael and Michelangelo are hard to imagine: the mere fact of the difference in the length of their working lives (Raphael's active career lasted twenty years, Michelangelo's closer to seventy five), let alone their widely divergent personalities, already contrasted by contemporary critics, seems to render detailed comparison absurd. Yet there are obvious points of contact, for both artists enjoyed the patronage of successive Popes, and paid the price for it in terms of labouring under intense pressure of work with the concomitant frustration of seeing challenging projects left incomplete – for instance Raphael was apparently thwarted at an advanced stage in his preparation for a major Roman altarpiece (see No. 21) while much of Michelangelo's career was shadowed by the impossibility of realizing his grand vision of the tomb of Julius II. Pressure of work had different effects: Raphael painted less and less as he directed his efficient studio to carry out a variety of work, while the more solitary Michelangelo, for whom delegation was anathema, must have vicariously enjoyed seeing his friends successfully complete their own commissions with the help of his designs.

Above all, it is in the drawings of Raphael and Michelangelo that comparisons and contrasts can be illuminating. They both looked to Leonardo, who had pioneered new drawing techniques, and his achievements acted as a stimulus to Michelangelo and Raphael, in whose hands drawing practice and the status of drawing itself were transformed. In different ways, their drawings can aspire to the same expressive and affecting ends as painting or sculpture, rather than being simply professional tools. Thus Raphael attached prime importance to bringing his ideas to complete fruition on paper, so much so that perfection of a kind, in a monochrome medium, results at the final preparatory stage, which is impossible to reproduce exactly in coloured pigments. He also used drawing as a means of bringing his skills to the eyes of a wide audience, not only allowing the engraver Marcantonio Raimondi to reproduce his drawings (some revealing compositional designs which were to be altered in the final painting) but more significantly designing a virtuoso piece, the *Massacre of the Innocents* (c.1511) combining drama and pathos in a complex narrative, purely for circulation as a print. Michelangelo made subtly worked drawings of *teste divine,* ideal heads, or of allegorical subjects, as independent works of art which he gave as gifts to his intimates, gifts to be prized for their expressiveness and skill. In his old age, his drawings chart a spiritual pilgrimage more fully than his late marbles. With both artists, technical mastery is brought to new heights, with drawings serving as exemplars for pupils and followers (sometimes being ruined through over-use: Michelangelo's splendid cartoon for the projected *Battle of Cascina* fresco was more or less destroyed by the manhandling of eager copyists). Both artists develop a freedom and spontaneity in grappling with ideas on paper, based on a knowledge of the potential of tools and materials which goes far beyond the hard-won skills of Quattrocento drawing practice, though early training left its mark on each.

Aristotile da Sangallo after Michelangelo *The Battle of Cascina.* Oil on panel, 76.4 × 130.2 cm. Holkham Hall, Norfolk.

Marcantonio Raimondi after Raphael *The Massacre of the Innocents.* Engraving. British Museum.

How the drawings of Michelangelo and Raphael survived beyond their lifetimes, and the way in which they were appreciated by other artists and sought after by collectors, is too complicated a story to tell here. One of the most important groups of Raphael drawings in existence, and a major collection of Michelangelo drawings are held by the University of Oxford in the Ashmolean Museum, thanks to chance and the generosity of benefactors. Essentially, owing to the sale of many Italian collections in the 18th and early 19th centuries, including those belonging to the descendents of Timoteo Viti (an assistant of Raphael who held most of his drawings from the studio), and of Leonardo Buonarroti, Michelangelo's nephew and heir, one of the greatest collections of drawings in Europe was amassed by Sir Thomas Lawrence. He wished his drawings to go to the nation, but as the government was unwilling to purchase them at his death in 1830, some of Lawrence's collection was sold. The University became somewhat reluctantly involved, thanks chiefly to the interest and enthusiasm of the Revd. Henry Wellesley, himself a collector. The remainder of Lawrence's Raphael and Michelangelo drawings came to Oxford in 1846 as a gift by public subscription, the second Earl of Eldon having provided most of the funds. In this country, the British Museum and the Royal Library, Windsor, also have rich holdings of drawings by both artists.

This book attempts to present Raphael and Michelangelo as draughtsmen, through a selection of drawings from the Ashmolean Museum which are examined principally from the point of view of technique and purpose, but also to some extent for what they can tell us about the artists' interests and development. Problems of attribution and changing critical opinions about the drawings are not dealt with, and for this the reader should consult the authorities listed on p.80. The drawings are grouped under different headings so that comparisons can be made between the two artists' procedures and purposes. Although a considerable portion of Michelangelo's *oeuvre* is architectural, and Raphael too was active and influential in this sphere, architectural drawings have not been included because they form a distinctive category which would require a lengthier study than the limited space of this book could allow.

The drawings discussed in this book all have a P.II number, a reference to Parker's catalogue listed on p.80. In many cases Robinson's views are mentioned or quoted, and the reader will find these in the work also listed on p.80.

Raphael in Umbria

1   Studies for a guard in a _Resurrection_ and of an angel
Metalpoint, heightened with white bodycolour, on a greyish-green preparation. 32.7 × 23.6 cm
P.II 506

Vasari said that it was often difficult to distinguish Raphael's early works from those of Perugino, a remark which still holds true. Raphael had a close association with Perugino and his workshop which continued even while he worked as an independent master from c.1499. His distinctive character shows through in drawings such as No. 1, made from the life, where a _garzone_ or studio apprentice would pose in everyday dress. The reclining figure in this and a figure in motion in another Oxford drawing (P.II 505) correspond with those of two guards in a small _Resurrection_ from the studio of Perugino c.1502, now in the São Paolo Museum, Brazil, so that Raphael may have worked on some of the initial designs for that painting. This role as a generator of ideas which others would then execute is one which Raphael slipped into early in his career (see No. 2). The kneeling figure, with curving lines outlining wings behind, need not be connected with the _Resurrection_. However, the angel apparently holds some of the instruments of the Passion (the Nails and the Rod or Spear), and such figures can occur in a _Resurrection_. Raphael's concern here was with the elucidation of the angle of the head and the consequent foreshortening of the features – there is an alternative discarded idea also on the sheet. The lower figure was begun on a slightly smaller scale but then enlarged, and Raphael endowed it with solidity through precise hatching and the contrasting value of the white. Despite his simplified geometric approach, Raphael displays a keenness to capture tension and weight in vigorously worked contours. By comparison Perugino's elegant _garzone_ studies for his _Tobias and the Angel_ of c.1496 (now in the National Gallery, London) are at a further remove from the human form. Nevertheless this type of life study, especially in its emphasis on the details of heads and hands, was fundamental to Raphael's Umbrian training.

Perugino _Studies for 'Tobias and the Angel'._ Metalpoint heightened with bodycolour on a cream preparation. 23.8 × 18.3 cm. P.II 27.

Metalpoint: A metal stylus (of gold, silver, lead or other metal) drawn over a prepared abrasive surface which leaves a thin indelible line.

8

2   **A group of four standing soldiers**
Metalpoint on a pale bluish-grey preparation.
21.3 × 22.3 cm
P.II 510

One of Raphael's many gifts was that he was an astonishingly fast learner; this drawing, probably made in 1503, is a rapid and assured *garzone* sketch which breathes an entirely different spirit from No. 1, not only because of the artist's assimilation of the achievements of masters of taut muscular form like Signorelli or Pollaiuolo. Raphael experimented here with the poses of individual figures and visualized them in relation to each other, correcting with confidence as his invention took form. One can almost see the models moving in response to the artist's flow of ideas: for instance the figure holding a staff with both hands is examined on the left in an alert, tense stance, legs apart and head twisting back, and on the other side of the sheet in an intricate pose spiralling from tightly crossed legs. Raphael used the sharp, precise tool of metalpoint with its delicate indelible line as though it were as flexible as the quill pen dipped in ink. Thoroughly trained in the Quattrocento mode of learning to draw first with metalpoint in a controlled, calculated manner, Raphael made this stiff instrument his own and continued to use it when it suited his purposes side by side with the pen, brush or chalks, after it had been discarded by others as old-fashioned and inflexible.

The drawing is a preliminary study for a group in the middle distance of the fresco *Frederick III bestowing the Poet's Crown on Aeneas Sylvius Piccolomini*, one of a cycle commissioned from Pintoricchio in June 1502 for the decoration of the Piccolomini Library in Siena. Three of the figures appear in the fresco, the central one and those on the left and far right with their positions transposed in the painting. Raphael collaborated with the older artist, according to Vasari providing many of the designs (four studies by him survive for the project) which were then painted, with much elaboration of detail and some modifications, by Pintoricchio and his assistants. While some scholars in the past found it hard to believe that the successful head of a studio would meekly work from ideas provided by his junior, critics like Robinson convincingly argued that the pragmatic Pintoricchio would have been happy to avail himself of Raphael's obvious powers of invention, and pointed out that the finished painting with its additional detail was somewhat inferior in quality to this vivacious drawing.

3 St. Jerome in a landscape

Pen and brown ink over indications with the stylus
and traces of black chalk. 24.4 × 20.3 cm
P.II 34

This is a preliminary study, probably for a small
devotional painting. Raphael was interested in exploring
the saint's physiognomy and expression rather than his
body as a whole, for his arms and drapery are only lightly
indicated and the remainder of his body left unstudied
except for some indications of folds of drapery made
with the stylus and lightly with the pen. The contour of
the outstretched arm is, however, carefully delineated, as
the positioning of the figure in relation to the precisely
observed city view behind was crucial for the overall
design of the composition. The actual situation of St.
Jerome on a hill overlooking the river and city was of less
importance in this study than the decision as to how
much of the city to depict. Some indentations with the
stylus in the lower left mark perhaps the base of a cross
or plinth upon which a crucifix would stand. While the
top half of the city view, drawn over a black chalk sketch,
includes a number of identifiable buildings in Perugia,
notably the church of S. Agostino looming on the right
opposite the saint's mouth (St. Jerome was venerated by
the Augustinians as he had been mentor to St.
Augustine), the watermill, towers and river are added
from Raphael's imagination. The view of Perugia is
almost certainly based on sketches made outdoors, and
there is an as yet unresolved area in the drawing between
the real and the fantasy city.

Few landscape studies by Raphael have survived
(another early one is in Oxford, P.II 508a and b), although
landscape backgrounds are common in his work. On the
verso of this drawing are pen and ink studies of a church
on a hill and farm buildings, Raphael's first ideas for
details of the landscape background on the right of the
Colonna altarpiece, made for the nuns of Sant' Antonio in
Perugia and now in the Metropolitan Museum, New
York, perhaps as early as 1502 or as late as 1504. These
details derive from Northern prototypes, and Raphael
would certainly have been acquainted with Flemish art
through his connections with the court of Urbino. There
is also on the *verso* a light pen and ink sketch over stylus
indications of the *Madonna del Latte*, the Virgin suckling
the Child, a traditional subject showing the physical,
maternal care of a mother for her Son, which however
Raphael never depicted in paint.

4 The Presentation in the Temple
Pen and brown ink over black chalk. 20 × 20 cm
P.II 513

One of the most important commissions of Raphael's
early career was that of the altarpiece of the *Coronation
of the Virgin* (now in the Vatican Pinacoteca) for the Oddi
family chapel in the church of S. Francesco in Perugia,
which was probably made in 1503–04. This drawing is a
preparatory study of the main group in the *Presentation*
panel, the right-hand picture in the three narrative
scenes of the predella beneath the altarpiece. Raphael's
principal concern here was with the figure group and
with the complicated action of the Child being passed
between Simeon and Mary; the details of the altar are left
at a preliminary stage, with the black chalk underdrawing visible. The artist seems to have transferred this
drawing from another sheet where the composition was
first worked out, for the light black chalk of the altar has
apparently been sketched over pounced indications (as a
result of chalk dusted through pin-pricked outlines).
Raphael's working methods, already rational and
economical, became more streamlined as his career
progressed, and he regularly used transfer methods to
reproduce a motif or a figure for further study on another
sheet. In the final picture, some minor changes were
made (for example the height of the altar was increased
in relation to the figures) but on the whole the figures
here correspond in detail with those in the painting.
Although Robinson stated that the outlines of this
drawing were pricked for transfer this is not so. Rather
than being a cartoon from which the final design would
be transferred to the panel for painting, this drawing is
part of the later stages of the preparatory process.

Raphael comes very close to Perugino in this
drawing, not only in the composition (which is based on
the older artist's *Purification* panel, part of the polyptych
at Fano made between 1494 and 1500) but also in the
elegance of the figures and the stiffly-falling drapery.
However there is a vigour in the handling of the pen,
especially in the contours, and the figures are more
tightly grouped with greater movement in the composition, which altogether removes this drawing from
Perugino's orbit.

15

Michelangelo in Florence before 1508

5   The Virgin and Child with St. Anne
Pen and brown ink. 25.7 × 17.5 cm
P.II 291

This tightly woven group is vigorously and freely
worked, with the final deeply-scored hatching giving an
angular, faceted appearance to the figures as though they
had been roughly chiselled from a block. Indeed
Robinson suggested that the drawing was a first idea for
a marble group. The seated figure of St. Anne with her
head inclined and legs widely spaced slightly recalls the
attitude of the Madonna in Michelangelo's *Pietà* of 1498–
99, now in St. Peter's, Rome. However this drawing
seems to have been inspired at least in part by Leonardo's
explorations of the subject, popular in the Quattrocento,
of St. Anne supporting the Virgin who in turn supports
the Infant Christ. For Leonardo this theme provided an
opportunity to examine the individual psychology and
the formal rhythms of such a complex triangle of human,
divinely privileged and divine figures, which he bound
together in intricate relationships, striving for both grace
and naturalism. Michelangelo almost certainly saw a
cartoon, now lost, of the subject which Leonardo
exhibited in Florence in the spring of 1501 to public
acclaim. (The cartoon in the National Gallery, London, is
now thought to have been made as late as 1507–08.)
        In this drawing, the artist is less concerned with the
delineation of expression, or with striking a note of ease,
than with developing the inherent tension in the group as
the Virgin's body twists forward almost aggressively
with the Child tightly curled on her hip. This kind of
coiled female figure in movement is one which occurs
often in Michelangelo's work, as in the *Doni Tondo* now
in the Uffizi, Florence, of 1504–06, and notably in the
Sistine Chapel ceiling. While the drawing may well have
been made in direct response to Leonardo's cartoon in
1501–02, there are other arguments (partly to do with
some studies on the *verso*) for dating it later, and
Michelangelo may have looked back to Leonardo's
explorations when he was working in close proximity to
him in 1504–06 in the Palazzo Vecchio.

6 Study of a nude male torso

Pen and brown ink with black chalk. 26.2 × 17.3 cm

P.II 296

Practically none of Michelangelo's early drawings survive, except for a handful of copies after Giotto and Masaccio. Although he later insisted that he had learned nothing of use from his association with Domenico Ghirlandaio, Michelangelo's albeit brief training in the Florentine master's studio, which began in April 1488, equipped him with a flexible, dense style of pen drawing which remained fundamental to his draughtsmanship, and he used the pen remarkably consistently throughout his career. We do not know whether he learned to use metalpoint, but he did form the habit of using the stylus and leadpoint which can be seen occasionally as preliminary underdrawing up to c.1530.

Here Michelangelo first drew lightly with black chalk the main areas of the body he wished to study, shading in some parts. At this stage he was not interested in studying the head or arms: although the sheet has been torn and repaired at the top, a faint line indicating the neck and back of the head can be seen but no detailed drawing, while the penwork stops short of the neck. The artist's pen follows the movement of muscles in curving, rhythmic strokes, with very little cross hatching, which have an almost decorative effect while at the same time giving an impression of Leonardesque fluidity. On the *verso* are black chalk studies of a horse and two men which may relate to Michelangelo's ideas for the *Battle of Cascina* (see Nos 7 and 8). The study on the *recto* may be a close examination of the main *verso* figure's musculature, although there are some differences in pose. However, Michelangelo often drew on what was to hand so that the drawings, while possibly made at much the same time, need not be sequential.

The drawing might be a life study, although it is not clear where the right leg would stand, nor is the position an easy one for a model to have held. It may have been inspired by the artist's study of the antique. The way in which the *recto* figure is conceived, particularly the contour on the right from hip to knee, suggests that Michelangelo might have had a relief sculpture in mind. The figure certainly recalls that on the right of centre of the early carved *Battle of the Centaurs* in the Casa Buonarroti in Florence which, however, bends at a more acute angle and has upstretched arms. Perhaps recollections of his youthful battle composition came to the surface as Michelangelo began work on an important commission for a battle scene.

Michelangelo P.II 296
verso. Black chalk.

Leadpoint: A metal stylus which leaves faint marks on unprepared paper.

18

19

7 Studies of a horse and of horsemen attacking foot-soldiers
Pen and brown ink. 42.7 × 28.3 cm
P.II 293

These magnificent studies were undoubtedly drawn from life, and, just as in his life studies of the human figure, Michelangelo omitted the head or other parts of the body which were not relevant to his purposes. Few life-drawings of animals by the artist have come down to us (there are several fantasy animals, however, as in No. 31) although he must have made special studies when a commission required it. Unlike Leonardo (and indeed closer to Raphael's professionalism in this respect) Michelangelo did not pursue investigations of the natural world out of wide-ranging scientific curiosity; rather his interests were almost exclusively in the human form. As he said in a letter of 1547 to Benedetto Varchi, his purpose was that of *fare le figure* or making figures, summing up his interests as a painter and a sculptor.

The horse was studied as a preliminary to the *Battle of Cascina* commissioned probably in mid-1504 as a companion piece to the mural painting by Leonardo of the *Battle of Anghiari*, begun in 1503, in the Sala del Gran Consiglio in the Palazzo Vecchio. Republican Florence wished to celebrate earlier victories against the Milanese and the Pisans respectively. Leonardo's destroyed painting is known through fragmentary copies, while Michelangelo's work, interrupted in 1505 and in 1506, was not carried out in fresco, although his cartoon for the central group of *Bathers* is also known through a copy. This showed nude soldiers surprised by the Pisan attack while bathing, and Michelangelo clearly had in mind scenes of cavalry and foot-soldiers in the middle distance, as described in contemporary accounts of the battle, doubtless in response to Leonardo's painting which focused on the thick of battle with riders and horses fiercely clashing. A small sketch at the bottom of this page shows a horseman charging at a group of foot-soldiers; this is a rapidly captured idea which Michelangelo worked out in more detail on another sheet (No. 8). On the *verso*, with the ink showing through, are two sonnets and three love songs by the artist.

8   A battle scene
Pen and brown ink. 17.9 × 25.1 cm
P.II 294

See under No. 7 for the genesis of this drawing. Thin scratched strokes towards the edge of the composition reveal how Michelangelo first sketched his invention. These strokes were then altered and worked over: sometimes the position of a figure was changed entirely (as on the far right), while the forelegs of the horse were also altered. Michelangelo used parallel hatching and widely-spaced cross-hatching in a very bold manner, achieving an extraordinary solidity of form in what is a freely-worked, constantly developing composition. The hatching on the body of the rearing horse is most striking, especially where it continues over the outlines of the hindquarters. The artist's aggressive, exciting style of pen drawing here is perfectly attuned to his subject, which is inspired by the tumult and clamour of Leonardo's battle scene. Despite all its fierceness and spontaneity, the drawing represents a stage of advanced development from the first idea seen in the previous sheet, and it may be that it provided sufficient clarification for Michelangelo to move on to the final stages of preparation for the painting. As the group was to be placed in the middle ground of the fresco, the artist may have intended to paint it sketchily, and may not have needed to make a scaled-up drawing (which rarely seems to have been his practice) or even a cartoon.

  Michelangelo's keen interest in the work of Leonardo was to some extent mirrored by the older artist's awareness of his originality. Thus Leonardo reveals in his drawings his knowledge of Michelangelo's original plans of 1505 for the Tomb of Julius II, and later he drew the *Moses* from a preparatory model of around 1513, while he also made a free sketch from memory of the *David*.

Gérard Edelinck.
Engraving of Rubens's
drawing after Leonardo
The Battle of Anghiari.
Ashmolean Museum.

Detail of 7 on page 21

Raphael in Florence

9   **Studies for the Trinity of S. Severo**
Silverpoint heightened with white bodycolour on a
cream-coloured preparation. 21.1 × 27.4 cm
P.II 535

The fame of Leonardo's and Michelangelo's achievements reached Raphael in Urbino, Perugia and Siena,
and his declared intention of studying their work was
realized in a trip to Florence in, or soon after, October
1504. Raphael's interest in the drawings of Leonardo is
clear in this sheet of preparatory studies for a fresco of
The Trinity with Six Benedictine Saints for the church of S.
Severo in Perugia, probably begun in 1505. The head of
the young saint (with a faint halo) and the studies of
youthful hands may arise from an initial idea to represent
the elderly S. Giovanni Gualberto as an idealised young
man. The older head, a study for that of St. Maurus, is
based on a knowledge of Leonardo's profile head studies.
While these sometimes verge on the grotesque or the
caricature (many are deliberately so), Raphael typically
avoids any extremes. He equals Leonardo in the technical
mastery of silverpoint in the highly worked study of the
youthful head, displaying a keenly developed sensitivity
to tone. Raphael used a fine veiling of hatched lines,
leaving the cream paper as the light areas and adding
some white lead highlighting (now oxidised), thus
achieving an almost *sfumato* effect of shading. Raphael
turned the sheet around fully to make a rapid silverpoint
sketch in a spare area of paper. This is a copy of a lost
preliminary drawing by Leonardo for the *Battle of
Anghiari*; it does not record exactly the central motif of
the *Battle of the Standard* but shows the left-hand rider
with his arms bent under the staff of his standard rather
than over it. The horse seen from the rear just above the
skirmish is taken from another drawing by Leonardo
now at Windsor. There is another sketch, barely visible,
in the corner diagonally opposite, showing the heads of
two horses biting one another, probably also derived
from a drawing by Leonardo.

Detail

10　A battle scene with prisoners being pinioned

Pen and brown ink over light black chalk.
26.8 × 41.7 cm
P.II 538

This scene of wild and violent action is one of a number of drawings of battles (including one on the *verso* of this sheet) made by Raphael probably towards 1506-08. While the drawings are not connected with any known project, there may have been a related commission; also in some ways they prefigure Raphael's display of virtuosity in the *Massacre of the Innocents* of c.1511. In any case, the opportunity was taken here to explore freely the subject of the male nude in vigorous action and complex grouping. When Raphael first came to Florence in late 1504 his knowledge of anatomy was limited and he had little experience of examining the heroic nude. Like his two mentors, Leonardo and Michelangelo, he used mainly pen and ink for figure studies at this time, developing an energetic and confident style: here he lightly sketched the group in black chalk and then worked it up, with revisions, in pen and ink. Raphael's understanding of the nude by now was based on his studies from life, and on studies from sculpture ancient and modern (for instance he copied Michelangelo's *David* of 1501, which had been erected outside the Palazzo Vecchio in 1504, and he also studied antique reliefs). While the stimulus of Michelangelo can be seen in the muscularity of the figure with arm upraised to the left, in the twisting kneeling figure, and in the general theme of alarm and fear in the background, Raphael did not attempt to recreate a sculptural Michelangelesque group. Other influences intrude – the shouting, expressive profile head on the right strikes a Leonardesque note; the wiry, elastic contours recall Signorelli's nude figures; while the rhythmic grouping of pairs and figures in a frieze-like composition is derived as much from a knowledge of Pollaiuolo's fighting nudes as from a study of ancient relief sculpture.

Raphael was not a copyist but rather had a power of synthesis which made him the envy of contemporaries. Here his aim was to create a variety of poses of figures, still and in motion, with a coherent narrative and a unified composition. The ideas expressed in this sequence of drawings later found fruit in Raphael's designs for the fresco of the *Battle of Ostia* in the Stanza dell' Incendio in the Vatican around eight or ten years later (and many critics have seen this drawing as a preliminary study for the fresco).

26

11   Studies for a Virgin and Child with St. John
Brush drawing in pale brown ink and wash heightened with white bodycolour (mostly oxidized) over indications in metalpoint and red chalk.
21.9 × 18 cm
P.II 518

The broadening of Raphael's technical range in Florence is illustrated here with early examples of his use of brush and red chalk. If Raphael found the pen suitable for the study of movement and muscles, the monochrome painterly sketch with a thin brush dipped in diluted ink was appropriate for the examination of the fall of light on a voluminous figure or group. Robinson recalls that Venetian masters had earlier used this technique, as had Fra Bartolommeo in Florence; he also suggests that it may derive from the practice of direct sketching in a monochrome pigment on the wall or prepared panel prior to fresco or tempera painting. Red chalk, pioneered by Leonardo in his studies of Apostles for the *Last Supper* of 1497, was a medium which Raphael turned to more and more in his figure studies in Rome, especially (but by no means only) in those of the female form.

These working drawings are preparatory studies for the *Madonna of the Meadow* of 1505 or 1506, now in Vienna. Raphael first sketched the principal group with metalpoint or leadpoint (very faint traces are visible on the unprepared paper) and then began to block in the figures with a pale wash. The kneeling Infant St. John remains at this early stage, his body tentatively drawn yet full of vitality and character. The bodies of the Madonna and Child were then further worked up with layers of wash, including a golden-brown shade which adds warmth and density to the undraped forms (although there are some indications of the Virgin's costume). The red chalk drawing was made next, to explore an alternative position for the Child's head and His mother's hand, this time on His shoulder. By comparison with his vigorous nude studies, Raphael's drawings of the Madonna and Child are tranquil in tone. Although, as with Michelangelo in No. 5. he deals with a motif, ultimately inspired by Leonardo, of carefully woven pyramidal figure groups with a complexity of expression, no tension is apparent and decorum is never ruptured by unduly convoluted figures or by sudden movement.

12 Two studies for a Virgin and Child with St. John
Pen and brown inks. 24.8 × 20.4 cm
P.II 516

The larger study is a preliminary sketch for the *Madonna del Cardellino (Madonna of the Goldfinch)* of c.1506, now in the Uffizi in Florence, made at an early stage of preparation as the figures are studied nude. Leonardo had recommended such studies prior to adding drapery (which would itself be examined separately from models or plaster casts in the studio) so as to establish precisely the positions and relationships of the figures. Here the Virgin is seated turning towards her left, but the upper part of her body swings forward, protectively enclosing her anxious Son, while she looks down to her right at the young Baptist who holds something up in his hand (not yet identifiably the goldfinch). Raphael used a light ink first, tentatively establishing the main lines of his design, which he then developed with a darker ink, revising or reinforcing details where necessary. He was not concerned with light and shade at this stage, so that the rapidly-drawn shadings are simply shorthand indications of his intentions. His design was substantially altered in the final picture.

The smaller and more free sketch on the page is a quick jotting of another idea: with its scribbled lines and changes of mind (for instance in the position of the Madonna's head) it is close to Leonardo's inventive pen drawings. Here the Madonna reads to the Child who stands leaning against her (an idea further developed in another Oxford drawing, P.II 517). The new pose of the Child with one foot resting on His mother's derives from Michelangelo's *Bruges Madonna,* which was finished by 1506. In the end, the painting dealt with the theme of a reading lesson interrupted by the Infant St. John who holds a goldfinch (a symbol of the Passion) out to the Child, so that Raphael combined ideas from both of these drawings.

On the *verso* of the sheet is a sketch for a small barrel-vaulted chapel, or arm of a transept, which has no connection with any known project by Raphael. We do not know precisely when Raphael first took up architectural design, although he was very much involved in it later in Rome.

31

Techniques and working methods: Michelangelo

13   Studies for the Sistine ceiling and for the tomb of Pope Julius II
Red chalk, and pen and brown ink over some stylus indications. 28.6 × 19.4 cm
P.II 297

Michelangelo's reluctant acceptance of the commission from Julius II in 1508 to decorate the Sistine Chapel ceiling committed him to a task unlike anything he had worked on before. Few of his preparatory drawings survive: this sheet is particularly interesting as it contains studies for two major papal projects. The red chalk life studies were first made, exploring the fall of light on the *putto* who accompanies the Libyan Sibyl in the ceiling, and examining the Sibyl's right hand, which supports an open book in the fresco. The chalk is a warm orange-red, suitable for conveying the softness of flesh; Michelangelo used it extensively for life studies at this time, 1510–11. There is no apparent underdrawing, but revisions can be seen: thus the *putto's* forehead, cheek and chin were first drawn lightly on a smaller scale, and the initial sketch was altered or strengthened, while the sharpened point of the chalk was used to outline the definitive contour. Michelangelo worked on the shading with a variety of strokes and rubbings: the marvellous sequence of light and shade on the left shoulder and arm of the *putto* shows the eloquence of his handling of red chalk.

The pen sketches in the leftover spaces are connected with the papal tomb project, commissioned first in 1505 but interrupted until 1513. The ornamented cornice in the top left is an idea for the cornice on the lower storey of the tomb, while the figures are for the *Slaves* or bound captives who in the 1513 plan were to have been placed on the lower storey. In these quick sketches Michelangelo worked out the twisting attitudes of the captives with great economy, sketching first with the stylus the first two on the left. The second of these is similar to the unfinished *Rebellious Slave* now in the Musée du Louvre, Paris.

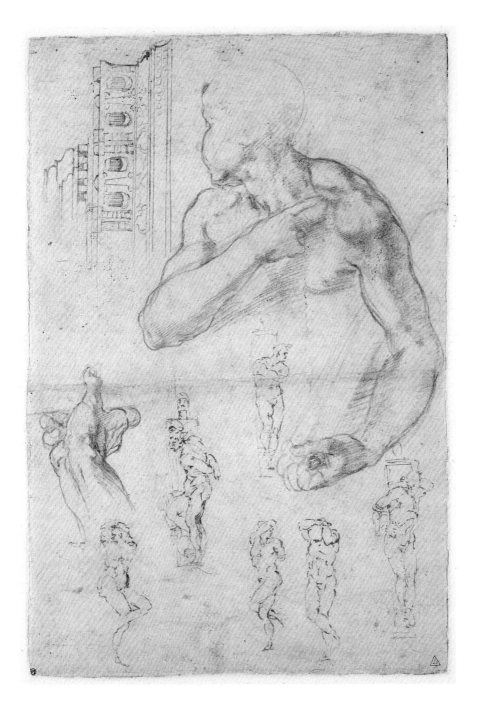

14   Two pages from a sketchbook

Pen and pale brown ink. 14 × 14.2 cm (top) and
13.8 × 14.3 cm
P.II 301 and 303

Both pages come from a small sketchbook, long since
dismembered, of which eight leaves are in Oxford.
Michelangelo explored in quick jottings, generally on a
thumbnail scale, a variety of ideas for the Sistine
decoration. As well as pen sketches there are relatively
large-scale black chalk figure studies on some sheets,
probably made from life, to work out from the first ideas
anatomically correct poses. Not all of the ideas were used
in the frescoes, but those which can be identified all relate
to the later part of the ceiling and particularly to the
Ancestors of Christ in the lunettes. Michelangelo
resumed painting the ceiling around September 1511
after an interval of about a year. The conjunction of
studies for the second stage of work in this sketchbook
(which may have been larger) and some other evidence
for dating the sheets to 1510 or 1511 show that
Michelangelo did not plan the details of the entire ceiling
in advance, but rather began making designs for the
second part after the unveiling of the first in 1510. After
that experience, he was able to work rapidly, and these
sheets convey the excitement and creative energy of his
working methods.

In the upper sheet the germ of his idea for the final
Genesis scene to be painted, *God the Father separating
Light from Darkness*, is revealed. Below in the centre a
faint sketch is visible of the foreshortened figure as
though leaping upwards. To the left of it a more
developed figure, arms widely spread, surges forward
with equally steep foreshortening of the head. Finally the
decisive figure was set down laterally with the head at an
angle and the arms flung apart as the body turns in flight.
Some changes were made in the fresco but on the whole
the figure has been realized here, down to the swirl of
drapery billowing out in the rush of air. Above and below
this figure are two sketches for a lunette figure connected
with the melancholy woman who weaves in the Jesse-
David-Solomon lunette. In the centre of the page is a
summary study for an *ignudo*, developed in a different
pose on the left. The lower sheet includes sketches for the
prophet Jonah, top left; for the woman suckling her child
in the Ezekias-Manasses-Amon lunette, and for the
seated man in the Salmon-Booz-Obed lunette who
appears there on the right without his pilgrim's hat and
with a curious staff.

15   Study for the figure of *Day*
Black chalk over some stylus indications.
25.8 × 33.2 cm
P.II 309

Michelangelo began in 1520 the project of designing a funerary chapel (the 'New Sacristy') for the Medici church of S. Lorenzo in Florence, to commemorate the *Capitani*, the brother and nephew of Pope Leo X, and the *Magnifici*, Lorenzo de' Medici and his brother Giuliano, the Pope's father and uncle. The marble figures of Day, Night, Dawn and Dusk which recline in pairs on the lids of the sarcophagi of the *Capitani* were mainly carved in 1524–25, with *Day* probably the first figure to be made.

This drawing is one of a number of life-studies for this large-scale sculpture, which would have required more preliminary work than a painting. Life drawings and studies from a wax or clay model were made so as to visualize the statue from all of its possible viewpoints. Michelangelo also made analytical pen drawings of the anatomy of muscles, and separate studies of details – on the *verso* of this sheet are red chalk studies for the right arm of *Night*. Essentially his concern in this sheet was with the way in which muscles move beneath the skin, and the changing effects of light and shade on the surface of the body, especially on the broad central area of the figure. Little attention is paid to the lower parts of the legs, nor is the left side of the shoulder and back fully examined, while the head was not relevant to the artist's purposes in this study. In the statue, the head has been roughed out but was left at an unfinished stage. The tension of the form has increased in the marble, for Michelangelo brought the arm fully across the body and raised the left leg further so that it crosses the right, an overlap which is already present as an idea in this drawing.

The black chalk which Michelangelo was increasingly adopting as his principal tool is used delicately here, and two sorts may have been employed as some lines are drawn with a sharp, pale grey stick while other strokes seem to be made by a heavier, greasier piece. There are traces of stylus underdrawing on the main contours of the legs and arms, suggesting that Michelangelo was working from the live model which he outlined on the sheet before the subtle working with the chalk began. By now the artist has moved away from the steady, precise hatching of earlier life studies (see No. 13) and instead creates a gentle film of grey punctuated by deep shadows and enlivened by the rubbing of the chalk with his fingers or by the addition of white highlighting.

Michelangelo *Day*. Tomb of Giuliano de'Medici, S. Lorenzo, Florence.

36

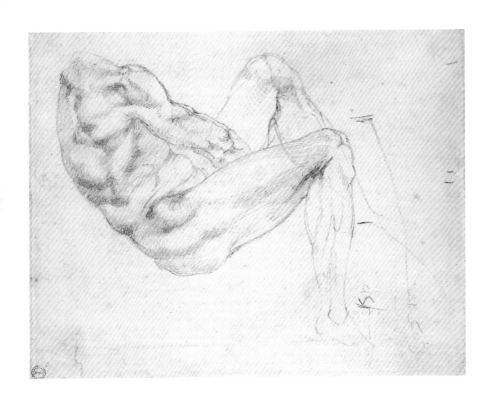

37

16   A man rising from the tomb
Black chalk. 21.6 × 26.6 cm
P.II 330

This is a working drawing for a figure in the fresco of the *Last Judgement* which covers the altar wall of the Sistine Chapel: the commission originated in 1533 from Clement VII, whose papacy had encompassed the trauma of the Sack of Rome in 1527, while Michelangelo's work in fresco spans the years 1536–41. The artist's first intention was to preserve Perugino's altarpiece of the *Assumption*, and his own lunettes painted on the end wall in 1512. Two important compositional drawings which have come down to us show an early idea for a fairly static group of Christ and the elect, and next a larger, more dynamic composition, still at an unresolved stage, sketched very summarily on the basis of separate groups of intertwined figures. Having developed the composition, Michelangelo studied the details of individual figures in working drawings made from the life or from wax or clay models. This figure appears, somewhat modified, emerging head and shoulders foremost from a tomb in the lower left of the fresco.

In this drawing Michelangelo's concern was with the heavy musculature of the right arm and fore-shortened left shoulder, so that the rest of the body is roughly sketched and the angle of the head barely indicated. He made a closer examination of the right hand in a separate study below. Black chalk was by now almost exclusively his medium for drawing, while in these quickly-realized working drawings Michelangelo used a shorthand notation (which he had developed in the late stages of the Sistine Chapel commission) of little circles to indicate highlighting, as can be seen on the right arm. The repetition of the contours was partly an act of revision and definition, but it becomes character-istic of Michelangelo's drawings from the late 1530s onwards. We know that the artist was long-sighted, and that this was intensifying as he reached his late fifties, so that this insistent repetition may have partly resulted from his eye condition. The *Last Judgement* is an extraordinarily powerful and even terrifying work, conceived in difficult times of war and doubt, and Michelangelo no longer sought to express an ideal of beauty in the forms he created. Even preparatory drawings as rapidly made as this have an eerie expressionistic quality which only partly derives from their exaggerations of form. Such drawings were not made to soothe the mind.

17 Studies of a group of two fighting men
Black chalk. 21 × 24.5 cm
P.II 328

This sheet of studies – once larger in size – was altered at an early stage in that the top right section, with some other drawings by Michelangelo, has been pasted in to replace a cut-out piece. It was possibly thought appropriate to fill the gap with motifs which included a figure with his right arm upraised as in the main sketches. In fact the addition shows figures drawn in a very light black chalk, almost like leadpoint in effect, relating to the composition of the *Expulsion of the Moneychangers* for which there are further designs in the British Museum, and which was probably made around the same time as those on the larger sheet, c.1550–55.

Michelangelo's ideas can be traced in rapid succession for this fighting group, which could depict *Samson slaying the Philistine* (although the weapon is not clearly the jawbone of an ass) or *Cain Killing Abel*, or perhaps *Hercules and Cacus*. A quick sketch at the top left was further developed in reverse on the right. Below, an entirely different viewpoint was considered with one figure straddling the other whom we now view from behind. Michelangelo also tried out a river-god pose, quickly set down on the left, which he then explored in a worked-up drawing where the figures are so intertwined that their limbs coil together in the centre in a wriggling mass, and here he went over the contours so as to distinguish one figure from the other. The group was finally modified on the right, where the air circulates between the figures and the attacker grasps the reclining man by the top of his head so that his expression can more clearly be seen. This is a carefully worked and finished sketch, highly elaborate and expressive.

Robinson suggested that, given the small size and careful disposition of the group, it might have been intended as a design for a medal or circular relief. This is always possible, although the scale of Michelangelo's drawings often bears no relation to the size of the actual project, and he was most reluctant to make designs for the goldsmith. While the drawings may have had a specific function, they may equally have been made in the pursuit of an idea without a project in mind. One of Michelangelo's assistants reported how the master would sit shoeless for hours drawing: unlike Raphael, Michelangelo left numerous drawings which are not connected with particular commissions.

Techniques and working methods: Raphael

18   Studies for figures in an *Entombment*
Pen and brown ink over black chalk outlines with
some red, the contours of the main figures pricked
for transfer. 28.2 × 24.6 cm
P.II 532

An important commission of Raphael's early career was
that of the *Entombment* altarpiece, dated 1507, now in the
Borghese Gallery, Rome. Atalanta Baglione ordered it
for the family chapel in S. Francesco in Perugia. Raphael
began with the idea of a *Lamentation* (and a drawing at
Oxford, P.II 529, reveals that he took as his starting-point
Perugino's composition for S. Chiara of c.1495) but
rapidly moved towards the more dynamic theme of the
carrying of Christ's body to the tomb. This drawing
comes at an advanced stage in the preparation: Raphael
wished to study the figures who bear the body of Christ,
laid in a winding-sheet. The stylus was first used to
indicate some contours, followed by a light black chalk
underdrawing, and next by a detailed observation, in a
network of shading with the pen, of the effect of strain
and weight upon the nude forms. Christ's body is
summarily indicated in red chalk as an aid to the study of
the other figures – a pen and ink working over of the red
contour was soon abandoned. Raphael may not have
worked from the life: the central figure for instance is
unresolved. Undoubtedly he had Michelangelo's heroic
nudes of the *Bathers* in mind, while a connection has also
been seen, in the close grouping, with Mantegna's
engraving of *The Bacchanal of Silenus*. However, the
close proximity of the figures was not appropriate to the
subject, in that Christ's body would occupy a very
narrow space, while also obscuring the carefully-
planned bearers. In the painting the figures are similarly
positioned but are more widely spaced.

Raphael's practice was speedy and economical:
once developed, figures were transferred to a fresh sheet
(for revision or for the addition of drapery), by pouncing
charcoal dust through pin-pricked outlines. Michelangelo
apparently did not use this practice in his preparatory
work, preferring to draw afresh each time if necessary.

R.V.

19 A combat of nude men
Red chalk over preliminary indications with the stylus. 37.9 × 28.1 cm
P.II 552

This magnificent study, made with a sharpened stick of blood-red chalk, was drawn in preparation for a detail of the *School of Athens* fresco in the Stanza della Segnatura in the Vatican, painted c.1509: the combat appears in a painted marble bas-relief on the left of the scene. Raphael made extensive preparatory studies for the decoration of the room, which was his first papal commission and his first major fresco cycle, the success of which determined the course of his career. The fact that Michelangelo was at work on the ceiling of the Sistine Chapel nearby acted as a further stimulus to the display of his abilities.

Perhaps Raphael knew of his rival's red chalk life-studies for his fresco; he himself had taken up red chalk in Florence but on the whole had studied the male nude in action with the pen (hence the closely worked cross-hatching here). The figures were first drawn with the stylus, whose indentations can clearly be seen, particularly in the more highly worked upper parts of the forms. At the same time, in other drawings for the same fresco, Raphael had fallen back on his own strengths in using silverpoint a good deal in preliminary studies of individual figures, details and groups, so that his extensive underdrawing here shows him wielding a familiar tool. Red chalk must have seemed appropriate for this study as its warm tone is sympathetic to the human form. A very roughly sketched shouting figure was freely drawn as a foil to the right-hand figure, perhaps as an afterthought as no stylus underdrawing is visible. Raphael's increasing command of the male nude is apparent in this powerful drawing, although his emphasis on graceful rhythmic movement and formal patterning is still stronger than his interest in individual anatomy and muscularity. The Stanza was essentially a private room for the Pope and his intimates, so that Raphael's talents were not visible to a wide audience. The preparation for this small detail – the only opportunity in the scheme of decoration for displaying his power of designing a group of heroic nudes in action, a *sine qua non* for an ambitious artist – may have stimulated Raphael towards planning his virtuoso composition of the *Massacre of the Innocents* of c.1511.

20 Study of a kneeling woman and a separate study of her head
Black chalk. 39.5 × 25.9 cm
P.II 557 *verso*

In Rome, Raphael's preparatory methods involved a range of techniques, depending upon his purpose. He had rarely used black chalk in his Florentine years, but he recognized its rich tonal potential and the freedom with which it could be handled as he worked on the Stanze commissions in particular. For the Stanza della Segnatura frescoes, black chalk was especially used for drapery studies and sometimes for figures: the very atmospheric study for the figure of St. Paul in the *Disputa* fresco of 1508–09 is essentially a study of the fall of light on a draped figure (and of the position of the head). In it Raphael achieved every possible tonal variation by manipulating the chalk in different ways and by using his fingers, so that the figure has a weighty, velvety quality reminiscent of Venetian drawings and also of Fra Bartolommeo's sophisticated chalk drawings, which Raphael certainly knew.

The drawing of the kneeling woman, swiftly and energetically made, is a study for the figure of a mother who protects her two children in the left foreground of the *Expulsion of Heliodorus*, a fresco probably of early 1512 in the Stanza di Eliodoro, the second papal apartment to be painted. Raphael here examined in detail the upper part of the body with its tensed muscles and complex folds of drapery; the black chalk is densely worked and rubbed over so as to render the effect of flesh and muscles in movement. The remainder of her body, with the child she holds across her lap (and a summary indication of the second child leaning against her) is boldly drawn, with the full spiralling movement of her form rapidly captured. The whole figure is conceived in a series of expanding ovals from the tight cap on her head to the broad sweep of her lower right arm and of the child's body. Raphael lightly studied an alternative angle for the woman's head in the upper part of the sheet, examining what effect this would have on the shadowing of her neck and shoulders; in the fresco he retained the first idea.

The sheet also includes a small sketch for a figure group in the lower right corner: this is a first idea for another commission of the decoration of the Chigi Chapel in S. Maria della Pace, which occupied Raphael around the same time.

Raphael *Study for the figure of St. Paul*. Black chalk, touched with white. 38.7 × 26.6 cm. P.II 548.

21 Studies for a *Resurrection*
Pen and brown ink. 34.5 × 26.5 cm
P.II 559 *verso*

One of the most exciting of Raphael's drawings, this sheet shows him in the grip of creative ideas, scribbling down one after another with astonishingly rapid penwork in a whirlwind of ink. A variety of figures take form in the heart of this activity, emerging to be re-studied as fast as his pen can move. The sheet is probably the earliest in a sequence of preliminary drawings for an unrealized project, a *Resurrection* altarpiece for Agostino Chigi's family chapel in S. Maria della Pace, Rome, for which Raphael painted Sibyls and Prophets in fresco around 1511–12.

Amongst the figures which sprang to Raphael's mind in these studies for a group of guards bowled away by the sheer gale-force of the moment of Resurrection were one not unlike the central figure in No. 19 who whirls around with his shield held above his head; a second holding a banner who is propelled backwards, the staff bending with the wind; and a third who is knocked to the ground, his left leg in the air, by the rush of wind. This figure is examined in more detail in sketches of the upper part of his body and of his head. Other figures

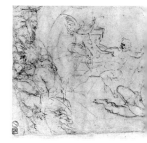

Raphael *Design for the lower part of a Resurrection.* Pen and brown ink. 20.8 × 26.2 cm. P.II 558.

on the page include a fleeing soldier, lower left, and rough studies of a reclining twisting figure reminiscent of that of Heliodorus in the Stanza di Eliodoro fresco, and of a Michelangelesque kneeling figure, which were further developed elsewhere. Another Oxford drawing (P.II 558) is a composition study for the lower half of a *Resurrection* including figures of guards based on these ideas. That drawing also shows a seated guard seen from behind which is studied in a careful black chalk drawing on the *recto* of No. 21. This is one of a number of relatively large-scale nude studies drawn from life at a later stage of preparation when the composition had been finalized. Almost all of these show the influence of Michelangelo both in the subtle use of black chalk to examine musculature and in the stimulation provided by figures from the Sistine decoration, here one of the *ignudi*. While the *Resurrection* project was abandoned, Raphael was not one to waste any effort, and many of the black chalk nude studies were re-employed in other commissions.

Raphael *Studies for a figure in a Resurrection.* Black chalk. P.II 559 *recto*.

49

22 A study for a figure of the Almighty

Red chalk over preliminary indentations with the stylus. 21.4 × 20.9 cm
P.II 566 and *verso*

A warmly-toned red chalk is Raphael's tool for this preparatory drawing for the central roundel in the dome of the Chigi chapel in S. Maria del Popolo, Rome, where the figure of God the Father was to be shown in mosaic, richly coloured against a gold background. Raphael needed to study the foreshortening of a figure floating above the spectator's head, as well as establishing the ideal character of the Almighty. Economical as ever, he first made a life drawing in red chalk, over a stylus sketch, of a bearded *garzone* in everyday dress lying on the floor, arms upraised, which is on the *verso* of the present sheet. Then he took a counterproof of it, pressing a sheet of damp paper onto the thick grainy chalk – a faster method of transference than that of pricking contours. This counterproof then served as a guide for the re-drawing of the figure (again first using the stylus for the outline of the head in particular) at a slightly different angle, turning more deeply into space, and for the more careful examination of light and shade. The process also allowed Raphael to distance himself from his original model and to develop a more appropriate concept of God the Father accompanied by angels. The figure here is now in the same direction as the mosaic. For the full-scale cartoon (to which the mosaic *tesserae* would be attached face downwards and then pressed into the wall and the paper peeled away from the surface) the image would have been reversed again, possibly by a further counterproof, and then enlarged.

Robinson wrote eloquently of this drawing, remarking that the figures 'are thoroughly Raffaellesque, yet in a certain austere loftiness of conception, and a powerful sculpture-like breadth of manner, they certainly bear a resemblance to similar works of the great Florentine [Michelangelo]', going on to point out that Raphael here anticipated Correggio's great frescoes in the use of foreshortening, chiaroscuro and the masterly handling of red chalk, although the purity of Raphael's style was evidently distinct from the particular grace of Correggio.

Verso

51

Compositional studies: Raphael

23 Christ and the Saints in glory
Brush drawing in brown ink, heightened with
white bodycolour. 23.3 × 40 cm
P.II 542

A substantial number of Raphael's compositional studies
survive. This drawing came at an early stage in the
preparation for the *Disputa* fresco in the Stanza della
Segnatura in the Vatican, painted in 1508–09, where
Raphael was faced with the challenge of painting a large
area of wall with the complex theme of a debate on the
nature of the Eucharist. As a study for a composition with
a heavenly hierarchy (Christ flanked by the Madonna, St.
John the Baptist and saints above a further tier of pairs of
Evangelists) this is one of a sequence of drawings
concerned with the marshalling of a large number of
figures into a majestic and coherent whole. The idea of
showing two tiers of sacred figures, as here, with
theologians in discussion below, was eventually replaced
by a grand arc of sacred figures, and the Eucharist on an
altar below providing a central focus for a group of
theologians. There is a strong likelihood that this
drawing was part of a larger compositional draft
(possibly cut in two by Raphael himself for further study)
of which the lower half is now in the Musée Condé,
Chantilly.
　　Raphael's concern in this drawing was with
establishing the overall tonality of the heavenly group.
There are no indications of underdrawing: an indented
curve on the upper right is presumably a framing device.
The figure at the extreme upper right displays how
marvellously free and economical Raphael's brush
drawings can be. Some figures were more carefully
worked, as in the beautiful fall of drapery in the left-hand
Evangelist, or the delicate white strokes providing a
sharpened silhouette for his dynamic companion. There
are a few marks on the drawing which might indicate
squaring up.

Compositional studies: Michelangelo

24   The worship of the Brazen Serpent
Red chalk. 24.4 × 33.5 cm
P.II 318

Few of Michelangelo's compositional studies survive, perhaps because his painted *oeuvre* is not large and there were long periods of relative inactivity in his career. Sometimes sculptural projects included carved reliefs, which might have required compositional studies. We know that Michelangelo destroyed many of his own designs so as to prevent his ideas from being travestied by others. Also, his habit of working intensively at the last moment for a commission may have meant that free sketches sufficed as a basis for a composition, or that, with his concept fresh in his mind, he could leap from jotted ideas and figure studies straight to the cartoon stage. This would have been temperamentally impossible for Raphael, who constantly had a number of commissions on hand so that it was essential to carry work forward in clearly defined stages.

This beautiful sheet contains two studies for episodes in the left-hand part of a composition of the *Brazen Serpent* (Num. 21: 4–9). We do not know of any related project in painting or sculpture. Above, figures struggle against and flee from a plague of serpents in an outward-spiralling composition. A muscular figure in the foreground (like the *Belvedere Torso* set on its back) curls up in agony as a serpent attacks its thigh, while further to the right a figure with one arm upraised, his body twisting in a typical *figura serpentinata*, defends another. The lower composition shows the edges of a crowd, where figures push forward to witness the miracle of deliverance. This more tightly-knit scene is treated almost as a low relief. Two men lift up a third who turns to look over the heads of the crowd: this recalls an idea Michelangelo first explored when working on the *Battle of Cascina*. This motif is highly worked, with the contours strengthened, adding to the sculptural feel of this group.

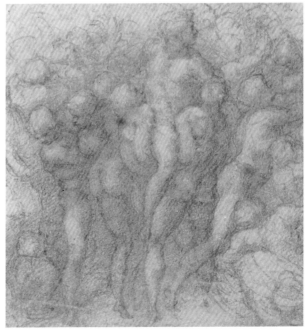

Detail

55

Drawings made as independent works: Raphael

25 A mother and child

Silverpoint heightened with white bodycolour on a
slate-grey preparation. 16.1 × 12.8 cm
P.II 561

This beautiful drawing seems to have been made as a
finished work in itself. In it the Quattrocento tradition of
craftsmanship, delicacy and control is overlaid with a
High Renaissance ethos of *grazia* – effortless ease and
gracefulness – and a formal complexity which also
embodies psychological complexity. The mood is one of
domestic intimacy while the composition is beautifully
balanced, recalling in its attractive rhythms and
intertwined forms the *Madonna della Sedia (Madonna of
the Chair)* roundel of c.1514 now in the Pitti Palace,
Florence. Another drawing in the same medium showing
a mother and child reading, now at Chatsworth, is
similar in spirit to No. 25.

Both of the drawings, which may have been made
at the same time, possibly c.1512, were engraved in the
style of Marcantonio Raimondi. Raphael may have
intended them as collector's pieces (although he did not
usually make drawings for this purpose) or he may have
had engravings in mind. He rarely made drawings as
independent works, especially once his career was well
established, so that his drawings almost always form
part of preparatory sequences or were made for precise
purposes. In Florence Raphael probably drew for the
sake of developing his skill as a draughtsman and of
exploring new ideas, for as he said he went there to study.
Even so, most of his surviving drawings can be
connected with known projects.

This drawing, which probably shows the Virgin
and Child despite the lack of haloes, has a compact
design and an air of tranquility which neatly contrasts
with the drama and narrative complexity of the *Massacre
of the Innocents* designed to be engraved by Raimondi
c.1511. Raphael went on to provide designs of mythological and allegorical scenes for the engraver, such as
the *Morbetto* of c.1512–13 (an episode from Book III of the
Aeneid) or the *Judgement of Paris* of c.1514–18.

57

Drawings made as independent works: Michelangelo

26 Ideal head
Red chalk. 20.5 × 16.5 cm
P.II 315

Unlike Raphael, Michelangelo did not make drawings for the engraver: his ideas were unique and closely guarded. His drawings were much sought after, both by other artists and by collectors. While Michelangelo destroyed many drawings to prevent them from falling into the hands of the undeserving, he also made others as independent works for an exclusive clientèle. These painstakingly-worked drawings were given to intimates as presents, testimonies of friendship and love, rather as he would write a love poem for a close friend. This idea of a 'presentation drawing' stems from the late Quattrocento, for it was also the practice of Mantegna and Leonardo to make highly finished drawings, sometimes after preparatory studies. Michelangelo made such drawings in his maturity: we first hear of them from Vasari who says that he made three black chalk 'divine heads' for Gherardo Perini in the 1520s.

Michelangelo used a warm-toned red chalk for this enigmatic head study, which was probably made as a presentation drawing around 1518–20. The chalk was used lightly and finely for the initial sketch, as in the rapid indication of costume on the figure's back. It was gently worked and rubbed in the subtle tonal study of the shadowed profile and neck. The final touches show the finesse with which Michelangelo used his medium – the sharply incised earring, and the delicate silhouette of the eyelashes. The figure wears a square-cut costume and a fantastic helmet-like headdress with decorative flaps at the temples, and seems to wear short hair beneath. It may be of a young man (although Robinson, and Ruskin, identified it as a young woman) turning aside in an abstracted, brooding manner. Michelangelo preferred making ideal heads to portrait studies: he rarely drew portraits except in the case of intimates like Tommaso de' Cavalieri and Andrea Quaratesi, and Vasari records that he disliked making portraits unless the sitter were beautiful.

27 Samson and Delilah
Red chalk over leadpoint indications. 27.2 × 39.5 cm
P.II 319

Besides 'divine heads', Michelangelo made presentation drawings of a more ambitious sort, with allegorical or mythological compositions. These were black or red chalk, beautifully and subtly worked in what was undoubtedly a time-consuming manner, and they demanded slow and attentive perusal to appreciate their high quality and virtuoso draughtsmanship. Vittoria Colonna, for whom he made a *Crucifixion* (now in the British Museum), wrote that she examined his gift under the light, in a mirror and with a magnifying glass. From around 1532 Michelangelo was intimate with a young Roman nobleman, Tommaso de' Cavalieri, and Vasari lists four drawings (*The Punishment of Tityus, the Rape of Ganymede* (now lost), *The Fall of Phaeton* and a *Bacchanal of children*) made for him as well as mentioning that the artist gave him 'divine heads' as guides to help him to learn to draw. Cavalieri inspired a good deal of Michelangelo's poetry and probably many more of his elaborate drawings than Vasari records.

The narrative presentation drawings often have slightly mysterious or enigmatic themes, or are of subjects which can have an allegorical meaning. This Old Testament subject is open to interpretation as a story of love and betrayal, or of the hero who eventually fulfils his destiny, but the artist here chose to show the giant in a tormented moment of recognition of the loss of his strength. The idea of contrasting a pair of lovers on a large and a small scale was taken up again by Michelangelo in a lost *Venus and Cupid* cartoon made around the same time, c.1530.

Michelangelo took immense care with the execution of this drawing, first indicating the contours of the great figure of Samson with leadpoint (visible in the contours of his right leg and left arm while indentations can be seen elsewhere beneath the chalk). Then he worked with the orange-red chalk either lightly and delicately, as in Delilah's upraised arm, or closely and precisely in the curved hatching lines of the shadows of the flesh. This careful shading in a mesh of loops and curls, as though Michelangelo's own fingerprints had softly marked the surface, conveys extraordinarily well the texture of flesh.

The master and the pupils: Raphael and his studio

28 **Psyche presenting to Venus the vase of Proserpine**
Pen and brown ink over red chalk. 10.5 × 8 cm
P.II 655

Raphael *Venus and Psyche.*
Red chalk. 26.3 × 19.7 cm.
Musée du Louvre.

Raphael trained a generation of artists who were able to work from his designs and execute the greater part of the major projects. 'School of Raphael' means more than a circle of pupils: his busy studio was a highly disciplined training ground where the study of drawings was paramount. Raphael's figure studies provided models for his pupils to copy so as to learn how to handle red or black chalk and how to render the human form correctly. By 1517 or so, Raphael's principal assistants were so adept at working in his style that distinctions between individual hands become difficult. Delegation of work was vital to meet the pressure of commissions, and particular talents were put to good use: Gianfrancesco Penni seems to have concentrated on producing finished compositional drafts from Raphael's initial ideas, which the master would then correct, while Giulio Romano was best at producing finished figure studies.

   In the case of the Loggia of Psyche at Agostino Chigi's urban retreat (now the Villa Farnesina) the decoration was painted in c.1518 by a studio team, while the senior assistants worked up Raphael's pen and ink sketches into compositions for his approval. This drawing is the only surviving pen and ink sketch of an idea for one of the pendentive scenes where Psyche has completed one of the tasks given as a punishment by Venus for her love of Cupid. Raphael attempted to formulate and resolve the placing of the supplicant Psyche with her offering before an amazed Venus in the awkwardly shaped space between the arching spandrels of the loggia. The initial chalk jotting beneath the ink shows the group on a larger scale and slightly differently positioned. Next, pen in hand, Raphael solved the difficult placing of Venus but corrected the angle of Psyche's head and arm. A few of the subsequent red chalk studies were by Raphael: in the corresponding study for this scene he made some modifications.

29 Two nude studies

Black chalk heightened with white (partly oxidized) over indications with the stylus on buff-coloured paper. 25.7 × 36.2 cm
P.II 569

The final Papal apartment to be painted, the Stanza di Costantino, had not yet been begun at Raphael's death. However, such was his reputation for realizing grand and noble concepts in his drawings (and for having a well-trained studio) that his chief assistants persuaded Leo X to allow them to carry out the decoration as they had Raphael's designs to hand. The surviving drawings include nude studies from the life by Raphael, as here, and some figure and compositional studies by Giulio and Penni which would have been made under the master's supervision. The initial work on the walls shows the strength of Raphael's impact on his pupils and also how freshly they carried his precepts in their minds. However, there were delays, and the oil technique envisaged by Raphael had to be abandoned in favour of fresco, while as time went on the workshop diverged from the original designs and some ill-judged changes were made to the compositions.

These life studies were preparatory to the compositional draft worked up by Penni for the *Battle of the Milvian Bridge*, while they would also have provided models for Giulio's figure studies and for the final cartoon. The figures are of two soldiers straining to pull themselves into a boat, and in the fresco their positions are transposed. Raphael's interest in Leonardo was renewed now, particularly in his search for soft *sfumato* effects: there is less emphasis on musculature as expression in itself. Here he first sketched the left hand figure with the stylus, but drew the second figure directly in black chalk having quickly repositioned his model. What is striking is the versatility and economy of Raphael's handling of the chalk: not only does he explore the fall of light on flesh stretched over tensed muscles, he also evokes the sense of wet bodies reflecting the water lapping against them. The shadowed profile, with the light dissolving the contour of the features, of the left hand figure is most expressive, as is the sense of desperation caught in his thrown-back head. The slacker companion whom Raphael envisaged clutching at the first in the fresco, seems already aware of his fate in the hopeless arch of his body. Raphael efficiently worked out the expressive and narrative role these figures would play in the painting, so that the drawing could be passed to his assistants as a paradigm of his intentions.

30 **Studies of the heads of two Apostles and of their hands**
Black chalk, touched with white, over pounced indications. 49.9 × 36.4 cm
P.II 568

This drawing in many ways sums up Raphael's practice as a draughtsman, while as a sublime work in itself it encapsulates his genius. It was made as an auxiliary cartoon (a type of drawing more or less invented by Raphael) for the large-scale *Transfiguration* altarpiece, now in the Vatican. The commission was a major one, coming in 1517 from the Pope's nephew, Cardinal Giulio de' Medici, in direct competition with Michelangelo's protégé, Sebastiano del Piombo, who painted a companion altarpiece, *The Raising of Lazarus*, now in the National Gallery, London. Both pictures were to go to the Cardinal's titular church at Narbonne, and hence for Raphael (much of whose major work was inaccessible to the general public) the commission provided an opportunity to place his talents before a new audience.

For many of his important public works Raphael had developed the practice of studying separately, at the final stage, the expressive heads in his composition, as a guide for painting additional to the full-scale cartoon. For the *Transfiguration* a number of such studies survive, of which this, with its additional hand studies, is the most important. It was on these crucial details that the full religious significance and emotional impact of the altarpiece depended. This contrast of youth and age, and of intense emotion, worked out in strong chiaroscuro, occurs in the group of Apostles in the centre of the lower part of the picture. The outlines of the heads and hands in the final cartoon would have been transferred onto this sheet (the pounced dots of chalk are visible where Raphael altered the contours slightly) so as to allow the master to make a careful study which would provide an exact guide for his assistants to reproduce in the painting. This practice illustrates how efficient and analytical Raphael's methods were, and how intense his concentration could be on the essential parts of a commission. (It is worth noting that from the copying of such expressive heads and hands academic formulae were later derived for the depiction of the emotions.)

The beauty of this drawing transports it far beyond its ostensible purpose: in it, Raphael achieves a profundity of thought and a power of expression which have been rarely surpassed in painting.

67

The master and the pupils: Michelangelo and his friends and followers

31 A dragon and other sketches
Pen and brown ink over leadpoint; red chalk.
25.4 × 33.8 cm
P.II 323

Michelangelo to a large extent was a solitary worker: late in life he liked to boast that he had never run a workshop. However he certainly had studio assistants, who prepared tools and materials, or helped with preliminary work. Many of these assistants' names are known but on the whole their abilities seem to have been limited. As their master, Michelangelo made some efforts to teach them to draw; his interest in teaching is also attested by his remark to Vasari that he would have liked to have made anatomical commentaries for the benefit of his disciples.

Underneath this splendid fire-breathing dragon are some weak sketches of profile heads in red chalk. On the *verso* of the sheet are two more red chalk profiles of which the top one is by Michelangelo and the second an attempt to emulate his command of form, an attempt which continues on the *recto*. There are also several studies of eyes, of which three can be identified as by Michelangelo, and the remaining eight as by a learner. This type of drawing exercise harks back to the tradition of studio model-books with motifs and details by the master for apprentices to copy. The *verso* carries inscriptions connected with Michelangelo's friendship with Andrea Quaratesi, a Florentine banker, which dates from the late 1520s. The pupil was probably Antonio Mini who assisted Michelangelo from 1522 to 1531. The magnificently coiled dragon, briefly planned first in leadpoint, is intricately worked with a variety of types of shading, giving the form a sculptural, polished finish. Probably for that reason, and for the craftsmanlike quality of its execution, it has been suggested that the drawing might be a design for an ornamental piece of metalwork. However, Michelangelo rarely provided designs for others to work from. This dragon may well have been drawn for its own sake, or as a piece of virtuoso penwork for Mini to admire and study.

Michelangelo PII 323 *verso.*
Red chalk and a little black
chalk.

32 Three men in conversation
Pen and brown ink, 37.7 × 25 cm
P.II 326

Although Vasari reports that Michelangelo burnt his drawings so that no-one would witness the struggles he endured to create his sublime works, we have little evidence of anxiety on Michelangelo's part to perpetuate the image of the effortlessly successful artist (an image prized by artists of Vasari's generation). Instead he saw himself primarily as a sculptor, depressed by the fact that so many of his ideas did not reach a finished form: hence his fear and loathing of plagiarism, and his self-protection to the point of destroying his own drawings. Yet he was very generous to those followers who were also his friends, allowing these other artists to work from his drawings. Sebastiano del Piombo, who came from Venice to Rome in 1511, was a particular protégé whose career Michelangelo aided by every possible means, furnishing him with designs for several important projects. Others such as Daniele da Volterra or Marcello Venusti benefitted from Michelangelo's grand concepts or his superior powers as a draughtsman, and it seems as though his help was finely judged with their abilities in mind.

Some other artists had access to the master's drawings without having him make works specifically for them. Battista Franco for instance was able to steep himself in Michelangelo's work in the 1530s and to incorporate adaptations of his drawings in his own paintings. This drawing by Michelangelo was carefully copied by Franco, while the two principal figures occur on the left of an allegorical picture by Franco of c.1537 in the Pitti Palace, Florence. There are inscriptions on the back of the drawing which allow it to be dated to post-1526, but a precise dating is impossible.

Michelangelo drew the elaborately costumed figure first, with some revisions. The second figure was added on a slightly larger scale, although the artist indicated his stance on higher ground, and, as a result, Michelangelo re-drew and enlarged the first figure's head. The third person was sketched as an economical afterthought to add weight to the slighter costumed figure. Hence the drawing seems to be a free invention. Robinson suggested that it was a vivid reminiscence of an argument witnessed by the artist. Michelangelo seems to have made virtually no drawings of *genre* scenes, but this, with its slight element of caricature, may be a rare example.

33 Studies of sleeping Apostles and other figures
Black chalk. 10.7 × 32.5 cm
P.II 340

This drawing was made late in Michelangelo's life, around 1556–60, for his follower Marcello Venusti in order to help him with a composition of *The Agony in the Garden*. The sheet together with No. 35 was once part of a larger sheet of paper. There is no direct correspondence between these figures and those in Venusti's work (of which there are several versions, the best being in the Doria Pamphili Gallery, Rome) but they doubtless provided some stimulus and presumably security for the artist. Venusti was accustomed to working from Michelangelo's designs and sketches. Some patrons seem to have been satisfied with a painting by another artist following Michelangelo's *modello* – Vasari reports that important clients, friends of Tommaso de' Cavalieri, were provided with drawings by the master. Thus one of these, Cardinal Francesco Cesi, had Venusti execute an *Annunciation* after a detailed drawing by Michelangelo in the late 1540s, while he similarly made an altarpiece for S. Giovanni in Laterano in Rome from a second highly worked design. In the 1550s Venusti painted other works based on the master's sketches including a composition of *The Expulsion of the money-changers* for which he was provided with a group of figures and compositional designs (of which one fragment is patched into No. 17). His work seems to have been much in demand, presumably by patrons who wished to own something as close as possible to Michelangelo's hand, as he would often produce several versions of one composition.

The tremulously drawn crouched and sleeping figures are explored in a variety of poses suggesting disturbance rather than repose. Many are conceived as compact masses, and would be capable of being carved from a block of stone. A grouping of three figures is studied on the right, in keeping with traditional representations of the subject. Two slight sketches of figures rising as though in alarm might represent the artist's further musings on the events in Gethsemane.

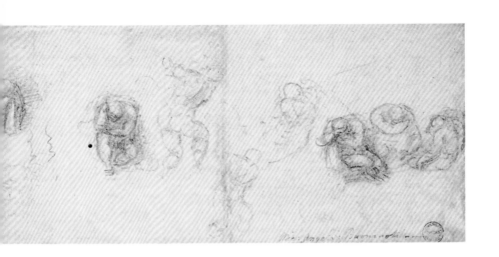

Michelangelo's late drawings

34 **The Crucifixion**
Black chalk and a little white heightening.
27.8 × 23.4 cm
P.II 343

Michelangelo's poetry late in life turns more and more towards themes of the tormented soul's search for peace and its desire for salvation, and of an agonized love of God which flows from self-knowledge and repentance. The same feelings inspire many of his drawings of the last ten or fifteen years of his life. Michelangelo had used drawing before as an expression of emotion – love and affection in many of the presentation drawings. Here a strong religious sensibility informs subjects, particularly of the Crucifixion, which in their obsessively worked black chalk technique seem to function as lingering meditations or even as vehicles for mystical contemplation.

This drawing is one of a sequence made probably in the mid-1550s, and there is another study of the crucified Christ alone on the *verso*. The drawings show Christ on the cross with two mourning figures, always frontally viewed. While it has been suggested that Michelangelo may have had a sculpture in mind, these do not seem to be working drawings for a marble group or relief (they are all on much the same scale, and show the same viewpoint, unlike his usual practice of considering a work from various possible viewpoints) but rather variations on a theme which had special significance for him. Traditionally the mourning figures should be identifiable with the Virgin and St. John, and the figure on the right here could possibly be that of a woman; however they may equally have had some other meaning in the artist's private spiritual imagination. The drawing is highly worked, with subtly achieved stippled shadows on the body of Christ, reminiscent of the laboriously concentrated work on the presentation drawings. The tremulous repetition of outline, and the brushing over of corrections with white lead which is also used for highlighting, give the drawing both a hesitant, tentative quality and an almost visionary radiance.

35 Studies for a *Pietà* and an *Entombment*
Black chalk. 10.8 × 28.1 cm
P.II 339

This drawing probably formed part of the same large sheet as No. 33, upon which there would have also been other studies: it has been cut on the left. The first two sketches on the left are for a *Pietà*, with the Madonna supporting the dead body of Christ, and there is a third sketch on the far right for the same group. The first one is forcefully drawn, partly obscuring in the lower part the faint beginnings of another sketch of the same subject. There are some variations between the three studies: not only did Michelangelo consider the group from different viewpoints, he also explored different expressive possibilities. Thus the first sketch on the left shows the Madonna, her head thrown back in grief, struggling to support her Son, while in the more carefully worked study beside it her head is bent in sorrow over her Son's body; in the last faint sketch she seems overcome by the physical and emotional burden she bears. These *Pietà* studies are related to the *Rondanani Pietà* now in the Museo del Castello Sforzesco, Milan, an unfinished marble upon which he was working up to his death, having begun it around 1552 and altered it at many different stages. The other lightly drawn studies are for a *Deposition*, with Christ's body carried by two followers, and these are possibly ideas for the *Palestrina Pietà* now in the Accademia, Florence, of c.1555. These late sculptures in some ways recall late medieval and Northern models, and some of the more expressive qualities in Gothic religious art seem to have struck a chord in Michelangelo's imagination towards the end of his life. He obsessively worked and re-worked his late sculptures, which are in a sense equivalent to the *Crucifixion* drawings with their corrections and repeated contours (see No. 34).

36 The Risen Christ appearing to His mother

Black chalk. 22.1 × 20 cm

P.II 345

This moving image, made in Michelangelo's last years, c.1550, seems to have served as a religious utterance or meditation. The theme is an unorthodox one, developing from another apocryphal subject of Christ bidding farewell to His mother before setting forth on His earthly mission, which was popular in medieval art; now the risen Christ, His sacrifice completed, makes a final visit to Mary. Here Michelangelo's astonishingly free use of black chalk conjures up through a film of light strokes the ghostly, floating form of Christ who (recalling the *Noli me tangere* episode with Mary Magdalen) almost but not quite touches His mother's outstretched hand, revealing the wounds of the Passion on his palm and breast. The Virgin Mary is a darker, more solid figure taking shape out of many revisions and carefully shadowed, yet worked in the same tremulous, sensitive manner which lends these late religious works a sense of fervent spirituality.

The drawing has been interpreted as an *Annunciation* in the past, possibly because of the relative positions of the figures and the fact that the artist made some bold, unusual designs of that subject in the late 1540s. However, the figure of Mary is clearly that of an older woman, while her gesture is not appropriate to an *Annunciation*, and it is hard to interpret the second figure as an angel. The composition may deliberately suggest that of an *Annunciation*, as the subject represents the severance of all physical connection between mother and Son, hence perfectly mirroring the earlier moment of Incarnation.

The inscription on the upper left, which looks as though it ought to have a religious significance, has nothing to do with the drawing but is a memo scribbled by the artist regarding his correspondence with the widow of his servant Urbino which was carried to Casteldurante by the muleteer Pasquino between 1555 and 1561.

Some suggestions for further reading

F. Ames-Lewis *The Draftsman Raphael,* New Haven and London, 1986.

British Museum, London *Drawings by Michelangelo in the collection of Her Majesty the Queen at Windsor Castle, the Ashmolean, the British Museum and other English collections* exhibition catalogue, London 1975.

J.A. Gere *Drawings by Raphael and his circle from British and North American collections* exhibition catalogue, The Pierpont Morgan Library, New York, 1987.

J.A. Gere and N. Turner *Drawings by Raphael in English collections* exhibition catalogue, British Museum, London 1983.

F. Hartt *The Drawings of Michelangelo,* London 1971.

M. Hirst *Michelangelo Draftsman* exhibition catalogue, National Gallery of Art, Washington 1988.

M. Hirst *Michelangelo and his drawings,* New Haven and London, 1988.

P. Joannides *The Drawings of Raphael,* Oxford, 1983.

R. Jones and N. Penny *Raphael,* New Haven and London, 1983.

K.T. Parker *Catalogue of the Collection of Drawings in the Ashmolean Museum* II *Italian Schools,* Oxford 1956 and H. MacAndrew III *Italian Schools Supplement,* Oxford 1980.

J.C. Robinson *A Critical Account of the Drawings by Michel Angelo and Raffaelle in the University Galleries, Oxford,* London, 1870.